LETTERS OF DIRECTION

LETTERS OF DIRECTION

Thoughts on the Spiritual Life
from the letters of the
ABBÉ DE TOURVILLE

With an Introduction by Evelyn Underhill

MOWBRAY
LONDON & OXFORD

© 1939 Dacre Press, A & C Black Limited

ISBN 0 264 67032 9

First published 1982
by A. R. Mowbray & Co Ltd
Saint Thomas House,
Becket Street, Oxford OX1 1SJ
This new edition first published 1984

Previously published by
Amate Press in Oxford

Typeset by Acorn Bookwork,
Salisbury, Wilts.
Printed in Great Britain by
Richard Clay (The Chaucer Press) Ltd,
Bungay, Suffolk

British Library Cataloguing in Publication Data

Tourville, Henri de
    Letters of direction: thoughts on the
    spiritual life from the letters of the
    Abbé de Tourville.
    1. Christian life
    I. Title   II. Piete confiante. *Selections*.
    English
    248.4   BV4501.2

    ISBN 0-264-67032-9

CONTENTS

INTRODUCTION   *page* 1

THE ABBÉ DE TOURVILLE: AN ACCOUNT OF
  HIS LIFE   5

   I. LIVING IN THE TRUTH   8

  II. LIFE   10

  III. OUR OWN DAY   14

  IV. FORERUNNERS   21

  V. ON BEING OURSELVES   26

  VI. AUTHORITY AND OBEDIENCE   32

  VII. ON BEGINNING WITH OURSELVES   36

  VIII. OUR RELATIONSHIP WITH OTHERS.
    EDUCATION   41

  IX. BREADTH OF SOUL. FEARLESSNESS   46

  X. HUMILITY. INDULGENCE TOWARDS
    OURSELVES   50

  XI. SIMPLICITY   56

  XII. ON FORGETTING OURSELVES TO
    LOOK AT GOD   59

  XIII. LOVE OF GOD   62

XIV.	CONFIDENCE IN GOD	65
XV.	GOD LOVES US	70
XVI.	GOD WITHIN US	76
XVII.	INTERIOR DIFFICULTIES	81
XVIII.	SUFFERING	87
XIX.	ILLNESS	95
XX.	DEATH	100

INTRODUCTION

THERE is a temper of soul which seems peculiar to the great French teachers of the spiritual life. It is marked by a twofold realism. On the one hand by a vivid sense of the presence and transcendence of God, a confident self-giving to God, as the essence of religion. On the other hand by an acceptance of human nature as it really is, in its limitations and weakness, and a determination to find the raw material of its sanctification in the homely circumstances of everyday life; yet without any reduction of the splendour of its supernatural destiny. The emphasis in fact lies on the Reality of God, His intimate and overruling action; and on that humble acceptance of the facts of our situation which Baron von Hügel called a 'creaturely sense'. With this balanced and deeply Christian outlook goes a method of direction which is perhaps specially appropriate to our own times; a robust common sense, a touch which is firm yet delicate, a wise tolerance of human weakness, a perpetual recourse to facts, a hatred of moral and devotional pettiness. Of this school of direction, so mild in appearance yet in reality so exacting, St. François de Sales is, of course, the patron saint; and all who follow him show the marks of his influence. The spirit of one of the latest of these, the Abbé Huvelin (1838–1910), has touched many modern souls through his two great pupils, Friedrich von Hügel and Charles de Foucauld. But Huvelin's contemporary, the Abbé de Tourville, so individual in his quality, so refreshing in his entire freedom from convention, his vigorous realism, his sanctified common sense, is hardly known in this country. Like Huvelin, he 'wrote in souls'; and the whole of his spiritual teaching is contained in his letters. From one volume of these addressed to two penitents the little book of classified passages has been made which is already precious in its original form to all who have come across it, and is now translated into English for the first time by Miss Lucy Menzies.

The development of De Tourville's inner life is hidden from us. We can only guess at the disciplines of body and soul endured by one who broke down after eight years of intensive pastoral work, and was obliged to spend the remaining twenty-two years of life as an invalid; exercising, in the intervals left by pain and exhaustion, a transforming power on all whom his spirit touched, and never losing his noble optimism, his vigorous interest in human affairs. A reference to the section in this book which is called 'God within us' shows the profound reaches of spirituality which he achieved; and a comparison of this with his more practical teachings proves how well he had seized the great Christian paradox, and was able to hold together its extremes of transcendency and homeliness. In a day when all the emphasis falls on the busy saints, and on social action rather than spiritual depth, we need to hear that valiant voice saying from his bed of sickness: *'Le tout est d'être dans le vrai'*; and again *'Du large! du large! au dedans, et le plus que les choses le permettent, au dehors!'*

All that he says of the spiritual character of an age of transition—for the movements of history interested him deeply—apply even more to our own time than to that in which he wrote; and the robust optimism with which he faced changes, convinced that God was on the side of that which comes rather than on that which goes, was never more deeply needed than now. For him life, even as seen from a sick-room, was inherently splendid. It had its struggles, its pains, its obscurities; but essentially it was *'grande et sublime'*. It poured forth from the heart of God and led man back again to God, often by rough and mountain tracks which we must accept, like the Swiss, as the normal means of communication. It is inevitable that we shall stumble, and sometimes fall into puddles, but we must take these things as they come and always go forward. The fussy and timid walker never reaches the journey's end.

As to the personal direction which went with this great vision of reality, it too, as these extracts make clear, was at once profound and homely. De Tourville was vividly aware of man's twofold nature; the life of grace co-existing with the life of nature, but never suppressing it. Hence his dislike of a rigorous perfectionism, his constant recourse to the standards of common sense, his advice to learn to laugh at our own interior hurly-burly, to show towards our own weaknesses something of that gentleness and tolerance which God shows towards those imperfect creatures who are the peculiar objects of His love. We are to take ourselves as we are; and offer ourselves as we are to the purposes of God. Nor is any one to suppose that this apparently genial method of direction, this avoidance of severity and entire confidence in the divine generosity, will lead to a slackness and indifference of soul. On the contrary, it is of all methods the most exacting, because it can and must be applied at every moment to every incident of every-day life. It does not require a special spiritual *mise-en-scène*, a peculiar religious technique; but works itself out, as did that mystery of the Incarnation upon which it depends, in the humble circumstances of our human experience.

Evelyn Underhill.

THE ABBE DE TOURVILLE

AN ACCOUNT OF HIS LIFE FROM THE PREFACE OF HIS BOOK *PIÉTÉ CONFIANTE*

The Abbé Henri de Tourville was born in Paris on March 19, 1842, and died at the Castle of Tourville near Pont-Audemer on March 5, 1903.

His father, who practised as an advocate before the *Cour de Cassation and Conseil d'État*, took personal charge of his son's early education, though he was afterwards trained in philosophy and religion by the Abbé, (afterwards Cardinal), Foulon. After reading law for three years, following the curriculum of the *École des Chartes*, he entered the seminary of Saint-Sulpice. Ordained priest on June 7, 1873, and appointed *Vicaire* of St. Augustine's, he spent himself with such absolute devotion as a confessor that his health, already shaken by his intensive studies at College, broke down altogether and he was obliged to resign his office. After trying for some time to continue to live in Paris, he was forced to retire to the country. There he lived in retirement for the rest of his life, partly at the family Castle of Tourville, partly with friends at the Manor of Calmont between Dieppe and Arques-la-Bataille.

The time has not yet come to tell the story of his life, which had in any case little outward incident, nor to disclose the profound influence he exercised on his friends and disciples and through them on numbers of people who hardly knew of his existence. Both by letters and by the prolonged visits he received at Tourville and Calmont, he worked with a success which the future may disclose, on the one hand for the advancement of social science, following the methods of observation he had been taught at Le Play and which he had perfected, and on the other for the advancement of souls in the true understanding of religion and in the confident practice of the Love of God.

The book from which the following extracts are taken is called *Piété Confiante* and consists of Letters of Direction written by the Abbé during the last twenty years of his life. The book was eagerly welcomed and hundreds of people found light and comfort in it. But some of its readers wondered whether its influence might not be more widely and deeply exercised if the chief thoughts of those letters were grouped together under general headings and all merely personal details omitted.

That is the explanation of this little book. It is sent forth in the hope that it may be of use to many perplexed and anxious souls. May it help us to understand better that in spite of all our weaknesses and sufferings, human life yet remains a masterpiece of Divine Love.

TRANSLATOR'S NOTE

The Abbe Maubec, of Saint-Jean-Eudes, Rouen, who compiled this book from the French original, has most generously given his permission for the publication of an English version, which I have made with the kind and constant help of my friend, Mrs. R. V. Vernon, to whom I take this opportunity of offering my grateful thanks.

LUCY MENZIES.

I

LIVING IN THE TRUTH

EVERYTHING consists in living in the Truth; once there our work is sure to be good, however hostile men may seem of it. Our Lord Himself, St. Peter and St. Paul themselves, appeared to have been defeated. Nevertheless, their work stands, and apart from that which has accidentally been added from the human side, now this, now that, it outclasses everything else and remains the final word as to the real state of the human race. There is no power—I do not mean merely personal—but no effective power in the whole course of things, except that which is in the Truth.

So you must be satisfied with being in the Truth, there to do what you can, however little or unfruitful it may seem to you; you can do nothing better: no one in the world could do anything better.

Never follow any narrow way; but on the contrary choose the broadest, the most generous way. That is the only one for you, the only one which will lead you into the Truth. And apart from that, there is nothing good.

Go straight ahead then and reach your true equilibrium through that tranquil and wholly generous instinct which brings back nature as God created it, to take its rightful position in this world.

. Let us be able to depend quietly on ourselves. Let us gladly judge for ourselves which things most help, guide, and teach us, by observing the degree in which they fit our own particular temperament; learning by experience those things which help us and which we most need. And then do not let us trouble about anything else. We may be quite sure that when we are thus following our own true line of development, we shall actually be fitting in with conventional rules and with other people as far as it is possible. For when we are being true to ourselves, we are in the best relationship we can reasonably expect to be in with everything else.

Let us be patient and persevering in our aspirations. Everything will be accomplished in time and will come right in the long run.

II
LIFE

EVERY day I realize more and more fully that life is a battle; a real field of battle. But also that God Himself gives His soldiers courage and a love of their calling.

This great and glorious condition of life which makes us liken it, not perhaps to a battle, but to a battle-field on which we do not know who will be struck down nor how: this should determine us to show the simple courage of the true soldier; resigned yet never downcast nor gloomy. In this respect you are trained for war, since you have seen so many of those you loved struck down. Of those who have left you such happy memories, say as they say in the army 'they died on the field of honour'. Life is easily the first of all fields of honour. We are sent to it by God and we are not recalled from it save by Him. On it we experience all the hardships, all the loneliness, all the difficulties, and also all the unnoticed and trivial heroisms which are met with so often on military expeditions, and which go to make up the qualities of the soldier. Let us then go forward and accept this hard but glorious condition of our life.

What you lack from the human point of view is a clear and optimistic outlook on this present life just as it is and on the actual progress of the world just as it is. Once we have grasped this idea we are, from the natural point of view, easily consoled for our own weakness and powerlessness and for all obstacles, by knowing that that which is good and necessary for us and for the world, is in spite of contrary appearances, steadily moving towards its achievement. We are like the crippled soldier of a great army, who, though disabled, consoles himself for being left behind by the thought that the army, in spite of his falling out, pursues its gallant and victorious march. On the natural level life is good, very good. Our own times, even from the Christian point of view are good and very good too.

Here is a great and illuminating principle for you: whatever makes life seem sad and melancholy to us is an error on our part and we must realize it. Remember this and act upon it. You will see how quickly you gain in vitality. If we find life unhappy and the world contemptible it is because we have not understood them.

We are all very ungrateful. If we truly believed that we are surrounded both by God and man, with more blessings than we really need to keep up our spirits, we should be both happier and more in the Truth. We should be light-hearted like those who always think they have too much, even when it seems to us they have very little indeed.

If you have really understood the Christian religion, you will see that it teaches us that God has destined man for the most glorious end; that of being lifted up to Himself, to a real participation in His Divine Nature, yet without changing the conditions of his human life, weak and humble though they be. It is a real venture, I had almost said a gamble; the most extraordinary gamble imaginable; 'raising the poor man from his squalor and setting him among the chiefs of his people, his own people'. For God leaves us in our human state, and when He openly does something for us, He still uses human means for His purpose.

Such is man! Such is that amazing creature who ranges from the lowest being in creation to the very possession of God Himself, even to the possession of God in this world by the state of grace. It is the vision of a great artist: bringing together and harmonizing within our good and reasonable lives that which is most lowly with that which is most Divine.

Life is a glorious road which leads to incomparable splendour, to the very life of God, to the goal of all things, to the full fruition of all that our hearts hold within them—as if in a broken but carefully riveted vessel of which the pieces though broken, yet hold firmly together.

III
OUR OWN DAY

THESE present times are really not at all bad though some old-fashioned ideas are apt to make us see the progress of the world as if everything were upside down.

Most good and even saintly people have the bad habit of incessantly lamenting inwardly over everything under the sun. I do not know of what Paradise on earth they can have dreamt, the remembrance of which makes them despair, for such a Paradise certainly does not exist.

Here in this world we make many generous and intelligent attempts, yet to all appearance they are usually unsuccessful. At any rate their success is small in proportion to their cost. Yet in reality the results for which they pave the way are enormous. Look for instance at the Roman Empire becoming entirely Christian on the very morrow of the most cruel persecutions; and this because everywhere the seeds had been germinating in secret.

Things go wrong in order to show us that it is God's will that we should change them. That is the real truth.

I think God keeps the world moving in order to shake us out of our old set shapes and bring us back to more natural ways. That at least is what happens periodically in history.

The present day is both very good and very interesting.

It is not right to groan over the state of the world as if it were lost. What is actually happening is a clash between the old spirit and the new, a clash which is specially noticeable because the old spirit is realizing how old it is and how nothing is looked at any longer from its point of view. It is a great struggle on which the issue is never in doubt, a struggle in which that which is coming triumphs over that which has been.

In this sense progress is the same in all spheres of life. In the world, in the Church, in the religious life. There is a struggle between that which was suited to ancient needs and that which is imperiously required by new and utterly different needs.

Most people are like sheep and follow, without much satisfaction to themselves, the lines of past tradition. A very small minority emerges, with great hesitation and amidst endless discussion to be faced by troublesome and pressing contradictions. It is however of that minority that you must be, when God has put you there by interior vocation and natural aptitude.

We live in a time of transition in which many things separate the present and above all the future, from the past. Such times are always difficult, but we rejoice when we see the light dawning beyond the clouds, clouds which have been piled up by ways of speaking, ways of judging, ways of acting, which are no longer those which the need of souls imperiously demands.

If shadows cross your mind on matters of faith, it is because all this has been so little taught in relation to our actual needs that we cannot always see our way.

In this century everything has to be remade, even that which does not change in itself. Take Nature, for instance. Has it changed? And yet you see in your chemistry and physics how the manner of knowing it has changed. Methods have improved and the same

things are seen more clearly. That is precisely what is
needed in matters of faith.

The absorbing interest of the present day is that the
world is growing itself a new skin. While it is true
that these solemn periods of transition are trying and
difficult in many ways, yet they have their charm,
because we realize that the heavy mantle of the past, of
all those things which no longer have any meaning for
our minds, is slipping irrevocably away and leaving
our souls free.

I want this to be your attitude. I find that it brings
peace and serenity to all those whom I am able to
persuade of its truth. The horizon broadens and lights
up instead of closing down upon itself and becoming
more and more obscure.

Social science will help you to determine the
meaning of this evolution. Put shortly, it stands for
the greatest possible use of liberty within the circle of
each life, so that no life shall be forced from its
natural bent, without some good and valid reason.
Our education is lacking in that irresistible drive
towards independence of thought which is so essential
if man is to rule himself wisely, in line with his own
true nature. He will not achieve this by relying on

current and traditional ideas but by the close study of every new idea, always joyfully shouldering the burden of his own responsibility.

How beautiful is this ordering of the social world and how valuable its knowledge—as infinite as the stellar universe, as ordinary as the lighting of a fire.

The world progresses according to certain fixed laws. On these all human changes ultimately depend. These laws, which uphold the whole race, are natural laws, as are all the laws of creation. It is from this source that all good ceaselessly issues; it is from this source that you and I have come forth, as well as all that goes to strengthen life, whether it be the life of religion, of philanthropy, or of science. It is this which perpetually remoulds everything according to the particular needs and means of every age.

All human institutions will in the future show less and less of this vitality and flexibility. In any case they generally develop on quite different lines from those originally intended. (I do not say this with special reference to religious institutions; it is true of them all.) History, when we come to study it, is full of such instances. But it is more especially true of the new and indeterminate world of the future, in which the speeding up of everything makes human calculations over long periods impossible.

We no longer pay much attention to the institution to which anyone belongs. We judge him rather on his personal merits; what he thinks and what he is worth. That is the present tendency and it is a right one.

God drives the natural and the supernatural world in double-harness, for He made them for one another. The actual, natural world is brought, by a combination of circumstances beyond the power of man, to a point at which it profoundly needs personality, diversity, original and contrasting characters. Grace, entering by the open channels of Nature, follows the same course, diversifying itself more and more that it may meet and sanctify this need.

Such is the true situation, accepted by the faithful and the religious. It takes shape and corresponds precisely with the providential march of events which bear forward the world and the Church and which in Social Science is called, as you know, the *Particularist Movement*. Because this movement has flung off its fetters and has lately developed through the growing importance of the causes which brought it into being, it is still a surprise, a scandal, a riddle, and a terror to many. That is why those who understand it and accept it frankly are in the position of pioneers and are looked on with suspicion by others. But that must not make us give way. And while treating others with reasonable consideration, we must nevertheless continue unperturbed in the path of the pioneer.

You were made for this; accept it quietly and neither worry yourself about trying to be 'like everybody else' nor be astonished that others are not like you; that can only come with time. We are not pioneers in order to find ourselves straightway in a crowd.

IV
FORERUNNERS

In every age God has scattered forerunners in the world. They are those who are ahead of their time and whose personal action is based on an inward knowledge of that which is to come. If you and I should happen to be forerunners, let us bless God for it, even though, living a century or two too soon, we may feel ourselves to be strangers in a foreign land.

Be content with training yourself in spiritual independence and let all your personal conduct be in keeping with such independence. This is the really essential point.

Do not be surprised if you do not win others over to your way of thinking. Those in whom any new truth is born have always to carry it for a long time in solitude. Even our Lord did not exempt Himself from this. He bore within Himself for at least thirty years, without any apparent result, without arousing any echo in Nazareth, the most startling news the world could have received.

Rejoice then in the light which you have been given and do not be surprised that it is so difficult to pass it on to others. It really is making its way, not so much through you or me as through force of circumstance. You are simply ahead of your time; it is a good thing to have long sight and to let your soul be illumined as soon as you are aware of the light.

Intelligent people can no longer deceive themselves about old systems and old ideas, circumstances having radically changed and changed beyond possibility of recall. Such people are in just the same situation as yourself. It is a situation which often seems hard but is in reality infinitely less hard than the contrary situation would be. For that would mean living in falsehood and driving into falsehood new generations who would be bound to suffer even more than we ourselves.

Be open to all new ideas and be glad to put them into practice wherever, as far as your understanding of people goes, it is practicable or possible. But where you find that there is no response or that opposition is aroused, then be content with your private happiness in being ahead of your times in heart and spirit. Do you not think that your beloved St. Augustine rejoiced greatly before the Lord to know himself in many respects in closer sympathy with the souls of the future than with those of his own day? Well then, follow his example. We belong to the Church universal; universal in time. And is it not interesting to see how in the nineteenth and twentieth centuries, God sends into the world souls like our own, which in some aspects belong already to the twenty-first century and in others to the twenty-fifth? We are as it were the first proofs of an edition printed only for connoisseurs but destined later on to be given to the world at large. It is good to be among God's experiments for the future.

There is nothing presumptuous in thinking or feeling that we are right. It is in fact necessary to get used to this kind of spiritual vigour. Otherwise we lose all clearness of thought and are bound to go wrong.

You say rightly that you are sustained, strengthened, and nourished by the interest and the kindness of others. This is precisely why we must, each in our own way, feed other souls. But as for yourself, you should not worry too much about this kind of thing. You have reached a stage at which you can get along perfectly well without this support. Is not this firm faith and absolute confidence in the way we are being led, which encourages, stimulates, and reassures us—is this not in itself an eternal earnest of goodwill? For, after all, what is this way if it is not

God's method of encouraging us, His special call for our co-operation? And again, is not this way itself due to the blessings which have, quite specially and intimately, gone to the forming of our souls? Is it not itself the outcome of the love of God and of all the supernatural love which at various times has surrounded us? And has this love not laid the foundations of our way, determined its character and gradually moulded it until it has become as clear-cut, strong, and definite as, shall we say, a tram-line? Joking apart, does not your way mean to you just what Joan of Arc's voices meant to her? Of course it does! It is the voice of God whom as yet you cannot see. It is also the voice of all those who are now either close to God in Heaven or close to God on earth, although possibly far from you now. They speak to you incessantly through books, through unforgettable words, through the inward awareness you have of their spirit: of that spirit with which they have inspired you, to which they are ceaselessly bringing you back and towards which you are impelled by their remembrance and their appeal.

You carry a whole world within your soul always. It surrounds you and you are impregnated by it. It has become part of you and since you are its creation and moulded by it, it lives within you. It is God Himself. It is the world of God and of those souls of whom, for various reasons and in varying degrees, you are the true child through the special nature of the grace which has been given to you.

Such are the gracious influences which abide with you; which uphold, cheer, and encourage you; which comfort and even applaud you.

It is they who urge you to follow without fear the path which with their help, has been mapped out for you.

V

ON BEING OURSELVES

Sᴛ. Tʜᴏᴍᴀs Aǫᴜɪɴᴀs says that the angels differ as much from one another as if they belonged to different species. This is equally true of each one of us. Each human being must consider himself as a separate world, to be governed according to its own special qualities.

God is working on you in order that you may no longer be a child, tossed about by every wind, a prey to external influences. He has given you your own grace, your own nature (in so far as it is good) your own distinctive character. You are therefore required to be yourself and not anyone else.

Live according to your own nature; inwardly without restriction; outwardly in so far as external conditions permit. I would compare you to a sailor; he has no doubts as to the port for which he is making and if he is obliged to tack, it is in order to make his port. It is not that he has changed his mind; on the contrary, he makes use of the changing winds in order that their very changeableness may bring him to his port.

There is infinitely less disadvantage in following the right road, even though it may sometimes lead us accidentally astray, than in keeping to a wrong road where we get confused, go round and round in circles and never reach any desirable goal in the end. Follow the route I have mapped out for you without being discouraged, even although you may sometimes meet with difficulties. That is only to be expected.

For the difficulties of a thing are part of its very nature. There is nothing in this world without its difficulties, and we must accept them with tranquillity and wisdom.

One of the hardest but one of the most absolutely necessary things is to follow our own particular line of development, side by side with souls who have quite a different one; often one opposed to our own. It is natural for youth to hesitate between an attitude which it fears may be presumptuous and a candid admission of inferiority to everything around it. But this hesitation must cease or we shall never grow up. We must be ourselves and not try to get inside some one else's skin. David could have done nothing in the

armour of Saul; he refused it and ran to fetch his sling
and some pebbles from the brook. It was with these he
slew Goliath, the symbol of the devil as the Holy
Fathers taught. Still less must we look for approval
and appreciation as a sign that we are on the right
path. There are not so many good judges as all that,
and the judgement of common opinion is far from
being common sense. Good judges are so rare that St.
François de Sales could declare, 'It is said that only
one in a thousand is a true spiritual director. I say
only one in ten thousand!' We must therefore free
ourselves absolutely of this anxious desire to be at one
with other souls, however virtuous or wise they may
be; just as we must never expect them to see things
through our eyes. We must follow our own light as
though we were alone in the world, save as regards
charity to others. In purely private matters, we must
never be deflected from our own path.

The moral and religious teaching of this century
has, either through ignorance or stupidity, given us a
false standard of virtue. It is a standard reached by
no one, and those who think they reach it are very
innocent and more to be pitied than those who lament
in vain that they always fall short of it. We have
forgotten St. Paul's two inter-related pieces of advice
(i) *Sapere ad sobrietatem*, which means 'be wise with
moderation' and not to excess; never straining beyond

our nature, beyond the grace we have been given, beyond our powers and our means. We are not to dream of perfection in the abstract but to try to achieve our own special kind of perfection which depends on our character and our circumstances. And St. Paul's second piece of advice (ii) 'God has distributed His gifts: some are prophets, some teachers, some interpreters' and so on. Each differs in grace as each member of the body differs in function.

This grand and simple teaching has now been superseded by one which is extreme and exaggerated, a distilled perfection. It is no longer simple but overstrained, made up of all that is most exceptional in exceptional characters. This standard is then set for all and we are told that there is no other; that there is only one kind of perfection and that it is therefore the same for everybody. We can realize what spiritual struggles this teaching provokes and how souls try to adopt a form of perfection which renders them as helpless as David would have been in Saul's magnificent armour.

We are the brothers and sisters of the Saints. They became holy in their way; we must become holy in ours, not in theirs. Otherwise sanctity would be for nothing but a wearisome routine for which nevertheless we could not blame such holy souls. They lived before us and did not absolve us from the responsibility of independent thought or of deciding for ourselves as to what suits us best. Why should we always give pre-eminence to the minds of the dead rather than to those of the living? What a strange method of progress that would give to sanctity! Why, for instance, in the religious life are solitaries not still trained after the model of *St. Madeleine à la Sainte-Baume* or of St. Mary of Egypt in the desert? . . . Come! Come! we must wake up and try to be that which we are reasonably meant to be and not that which other people have been. One does not become holy by copying others but by making good use of what is truly part of oneself. . . .

Every Saint is a pattern; but no Saint is a pattern of everything. The practical question for us is not to know whether they became Saints or not—we know that they did—but what Saints, in order to reach sanctity, have had to follow the path which God has made peculiarly ours.

Therefore leave your soul too, to pray as suits it best, in its own way, without strain. Allow it most of the time to remain quite still. Pray along the lines which show you the needs of the world and which interest you. Nothing could be better. In a word, follow your bent; your need of quiet or of doing nothing according to what seems most natural to you at the time.

When your soul begins to feel more at home, it will be easier to find out what is usually for you the quickest way of coming into the close and living presence of Jesus Christ. You will then be able to develop this special bent with greater certainty and will gradually discover the endless variety of ways in which it can grow. You will thus have cleared your path. For nothing is more individual to each soul than the form of its intimacy with our Lord. His earthly life, as it reveals to our eyes and ears His relationships with souls, reveals also that no two were intimate with Him in the same sort of way. Here again, observe the path you take instinctively at those times when you are most keenly aware of the real, actual, and intimate presence of our Lord. Realize that there lies your own particular grace.

VI
AUTHORITY AND OBEDIENCE

THE eternal voice of the Church has no other
function than that of giving the inner voice greater
clarity, so that we learn to trust it without fear of
making any personal mistakes. What joy and tranquillity this brings! This external voice has, moreover, a very special quality in that it is not only an
exhortation or a piece of advice, but carries its own
authority, which our Lord has promised to regard as
His own personal authority. It is therefore He whom
we hear, without as well as within. We are thus
wholly and demonstrably held by Him on every side.
Under such conditions how can we fail to feel secure?
It is surely because we always tend to revert to our
own ideas, easily convincing ourselves that this is the
right thing to do. But if it were, then the institution of
the Church, and in particular of the intimate priestly
ministry to souls, would become useless to us. We
should be in the position of pagans or Jews . . . and
should miss our Lord's greatest work. We should
deserve the compassion He expressed when He pitied
the multitudes because they were wandering to and
fro like sheep without a shepherd. The inner voice,
the very words of the Gospel, would become

uncertain and doubtful: we should be constantly afraid of misunderstanding if the clear and decisive voice of external authority did not put an end to our various illusions and give us utter peace.

How beautiful Obedience is. For it alone silences doubt, preserves our stability and presence of mind, our freedom of heart and firmness of will in the midst of all that might shake or disturb us. Unless we constantly bring ourselves back to Obedience, we lose our heads, and that which should be a blessing becomes a torment and a curse. We lose all sense of where we stand.

The object of all direction here as elsewhere, is not to refashion your soul on the model of some imported or prescribed interior life, but to direct effectually the powers and impulses which God has chosen to give you and which He alone can give. That is the meaning of the beautiful passage in St. John in which he speaks of the Good Shepherd who Himself leads His sheep, and goes before them; they hear His voice and He calls each one of them clearly by its own name.

The best directors are not those who are tied to any system, but those whose aim is to direct, help, and further each soul according to its own nature. For God never makes any two souls exactly alike.

As to your Communions, never deprive yourself of them except under an absolute prohibition from which there is no appeal, no loophole for hesitation. Otherwise, decide for your Communion and not against it. You need it. . . .

God never goes back on His creations and from the very first our souls are being prepared to receive His plans. Our parents, in bringing us up, form our first habits; circumstances complete our education according to the designs of Providence; our directors guide the development of our souls as a gardener trains his fruit-trees, according to their various natures. All this together constitutes our final personality, our individual make-up. It is this which we bring to the vocation to which we give ourselves. It would be altogether contrary to God's invariable practice in all things, if He suddenly decided to re-make us all over again from the beginning. On the contrary, in the plans of God everything follows in orderly succession and that which comes first is the foundation of that which follows.

We must help ourselves by the use of every good thing we have acquired on our way. We must never allow ourselves to believe that our soul is linked to any other soul in such a way that we rely solely on that external influence, on a direction external to ourselves. God wants to teach us to stand alone, without having to lean too heavily even on the instruments He provides. A child needs to be constantly guided, upheld, encouraged, and advised. But as he grows older his parents, who are for him the instruments of God, only really help him by their presence. They are available when he is in real need, but not all the time or for everything. The same is true of the whole education of the soul. We must reach the state when we know that there is only one thing which lasts and which is complete in itself: God, and the work He is doing in our souls through time and the sum of all the benefits we have received throughout our life from our childhood up. He alone is the Master beyond compare, and He teaches us by a series of intermediaries all of whom are transitory and all of whom, when considered separately are profoundly incomplete.

Once more then, love your only true Master, your Saviour, eternal and everlasting.

VII
ON BEGINNING WITH OURSELVES

W<small>HEN</small> we first become aware of deep interior changes within ourselves, the important thing is not to stir up and alter our whole surroundings nor even to attempt to make converts. We must first of all achieve our own inner freedom, and accustom ourselves to being alone in our point of view. We shall be strengthened in this when we find how unsuccessful the contrary attitude and efforts are. We must learn to find great peace in this personal possession of the truth.

Be glad that you can recognize what ought to be done, and what you would do if it were possible. There lies your real consolation (sometimes rather a heavy one) for being in the right way, for seeing the Truth, and living in and absorbing the Light. And, added to this is the fact that in each one of us the really vital thing is the actual state of our own soul even though it is impossible to communicate it to any one else. It is thus that God makes souls, beautiful in themselves, and rendering homage to their Creator because He has made them live within themselves. It is with such that Heaven is peopled; they are its ornaments, the members of that blessed and radiant throng.

The main thing is to act with vigour and determination. Immediate success does not depend on yourself. Sooner or later God will give it to you and you will then realize that your time has not been wasted even although, in your efforts to make others act rightly, you have wrought a change only in yourself.

Do not attach most value to external results, but to being yourself in the Truth; to being free and at home with yourself, whatever other people may think. We have been badly brought up if we always aim at producing an effect on others! And, moreover, real influence is gained in quite a different way. True growth lies in being content with ourselves; and then, when circumstances demand it, being quite ready to share anything we may have with others. Do not therefore judge yourself by that which others can

receive from you, but by what you yourself receive
from yourself, from your own personality, your own
inner way of being. Cultivate freedom of spirit,
spaciousness of mind: live in peace, boldly and with
tranquillity. Some day you will be able to pass all that
on to others.

The way of Light is indeed beautiful and good. Yet
in our day, how rare! We must follow it ourselves
without being misled by the fact that so few seek it or
follow it. To be ourselves that which others ought
to be is more important than to make them so. We
cannot deal properly with any one but ourselves and
even that is difficult. Finally, we exert more influence
by what we are, by what we become in ourselves, than
by trying directly to influence others. There must be
prototypes everywhere. It was not when Christopher
Columbus proved that by sailing westward he would
find the Indies, that he opened up the way, but when
he himself quietly set sail westward, with a small
number of companions and little support; the first to
make the attempt.

Rejoice to feel yourself growing and developing
within, even although your external actions are
sometimes thwarted. To be thwarted should seem the
normal thing and should not interfere in any way with

the vitality you feel stirring within you. Something will certainly come out of it. Desire and strive after any results you like and which seem to you good and possible (or even impossible) but never be put out if things do not turn out exactly to your liking. The soul grows in the midst of all this and, like the mustard seed cast into the earth, becomes like a great tree. And there is always some bird of heaven to rest, even if only in passing, on its branches. Then it seeds itself again.

The really vital element in all that we do, is ourselves. The life and the treasure are within us, vivifying and enriching us. ... Let us devote our whole strength to drawing on this life within us, pouring it out, or rather allowing it to overflow on everything, to produce whatever results it can. Or, like the Sower in the Gospel, let us go forth with our hands full of the grain of life, scattering it abroad, but not expecting to receive it from others. If they, in their turn, do give it to us, whether they know it or not, so much the better; we will profit by it, live by it, gain fresh vitality from it. Our concern, everybody's concern in this world, is to become generous and noble, not according to the pride of the world, but in simplicity and truth. Such action is certain to bear fruit even although it will not always be obvious. In any case the principle with which our Lord sent out the seventy disciples applies here:

Into whatsoever house ye shall enter, first say, Peace be to this house. And if a son of peace be there, your peace shall rest upon him; but if not, it shall turn to you again.

VIII

OUR RELATIONSHIP WITH OTHERS. EDUCATION

Do not be discouraged because you are not understood or surrounded by friends. That would no
doubt be very consoling but it is much safer to train
ourselves not to rely on it. Our education here in
France is defective in this respect, for we are never
taught to be surprised when people are kind enough to
take an interest in us. On the contrary it is the one
thing on which we count, and that is really too
patriarchal. You will gradually come to realize what I
mean and the idea is not really a pessimistic one. It is
simply the realistic understanding, practical and even
profitable, as to the most certain way of finding peace
and happiness. Yet while holding fast to this principle
accept all the help which is offered to you. It will then
become a real consolation: a kind of extra, good and
unexpected.

As for charity, which consists wholly in friendly
relationships and kindness of heart, it must be

reasonable and not overstep its bounds. We cannot play the part of providence to everybody. The measure of charity suitable to your dealings with your neighbours is generally determined by the relationship which good manners and good breeding have set up in the environment in which you have been born and brought up; for the measure of charity suitable to you will be the outcome of Christian experience in real life. The difference, in this respect, between the man of the world and the Christian is one of motive only; the man of the world acts purely from good breeding, the Christian for the sake of goodness itself.

Set aside everything which might make you at all touchy or timid and let all your qualities of goodwill, frankness, and simplicity shine forth in your dealings with every one you meet. Never mind how different their characters and way of life may be, for our Lord desires us to behave thus even to the unrighteous which would otherwise be difficult. Do not let us pay any attention inwardly to the wounds we may receive, but take ourselves firmly to task for being influenced by such things. Outwardly, too, we should ignore them and set ourselves quietly to think as generously as we act. In this way we reap great joy. 'It is more blessed to give than to receive'; that as you know was St. Paul's rule, taught him by our Lord Himself.

Encourage with discretion all that is good in your pupils; let them feel your support without being embarrassed or hampered by it. Education, as the very word shows, means helping some one to develop himself, to draw out all that is good in him. It is the greatest of all benefits. That too is the meaning of the expression *to direct, direction.* Unless interpreted in this sense, I like the word *formation* less; it seems to me to carry the suggestion of a preconceived form into which one is to force people whether they like it or not. But people do not lend themselves to this kind of treatment and so the form remains empty.

We must not bury ourselves in the gloomy thought that everything is going wrong; nor let it be a matter of indifference to observe which way God appears to be moving in order that we too may move in the same direction. This is especially important for those who are responsible for education; for the formation of those who will see the future and who will more or less make it.

In what direction is history moving at the present time? That is what I want you to consider. Which are the nations whose ordinary customs and daily habits are most likely to prevail? I mean, of course, good habits, for they are the only ones which ever prevail in the real sense of the word; the only ones which end in getting something done. When you have caught a glimpse of the direction in which these better habits, in the purely human and temporal order, are tending, you will then perceive to what good use the Church can put them for the benefit of souls. That will open a new phase in her history. . . .

Now, what practical conclusion can be drawn from the fine problem I set you here? Surely a most important one; that you must know what obstacles and what world-tendencies the souls you are now preparing will have to face during the next fifty years. If you teach them without any knowledge of what will soon await them, it is as if you sent them off on a journey to a country you did not know anything about. There are no doubt precautions which hold good for all journeys to all countries, but it is a great advantage to be able to take special precautions to meet special difficulties.

The souls we try to help, and especially those we try to bring to the true faith, are inclined to suspect us of only loving them because of the goal to which we want to lead them. They would rather—and quite rightly—believe that we only desire this for them because we love them. Love them, therefore, and without any hidden intention.

How supremely right you are in loving souls, whatever they are, for our Lord, and I would add, in His stead. For He has left us precisely this charge: the charge of giving others those outward signs, that sensible and visible help, that human expression of kindness which He gave to all around Him when He was on earth—where we stand now in His place. And real goodness surely lies in expecting nothing in return, while yet never refusing it if it is offered. To give in order to receive, with the intention of receiving, is really not to give at all.

But what joy there is in those gifts, whether they be great or small, in which we have been able to help or be kind to some poor creature like ourselves, in the name of the Lord Jesus, who has so earnestly asked this of us. It does not matter whether our gift is noticed or taken any account of by the recipient; he has at any rate received a good which came through us, through us from the Lord Jesus who is Love Supreme.

IX
BREADTH OF SOUL

FEARLESSNESS

THIS breadth to which I urge you, and for which I take all the responsibility, might lead others to slackness. But in your case it will lead to relaxation, to simplicity, to real heart-felt devotion. It will make you precisely that which you ought to be and will make you understand things precisely as you ought to understand them.

Think of yourself as if you were some one else, some one whom you have to help in carrying out those resolutions you have told me of, and which concern yourself. Do not be afraid of being as determined for yourself as you would be for some one else, if he were precisely what you are. Accustom yourself to this duplication of yourself.

Side by side, as it were, with the person who needs direction and reassurance, let there be some one very determined and fearless, who cuts short the doubts of the other, decides for him and urges him on, while himself remaining imperturbable, rejoicing in his resoluteness. This is a duty you owe to yourself. It is necessary to know how to treat ourselves as third persons in this way and to be glad of the discipline we give ourselves, just as we are glad of the discipline we give others for their good.

Let our effort be always toward greater breadth and generosity within ourselves, and, as far as circumstances permit, without.

We must return to good, straightforward interior ways and make use of them to enlarge our exterior outlook as far as we can.

You will come to agree with me that we are doing good work which will be of use later on, when we give time to the renewing of our strength; when we simply stand at ease and go as it were, on leave; while still taking for our own use any ideas which may come into our minds.

Believe me, a period of greater ease will be very fruitful for you just now; not only for the sake of your bodily health, but also for the health of your mind and your soul.

We learn much from the natural maturity which age brings to the spirit, provided that the spirit has already some depth of experience to which it spontaneously returns, and from which it gradually draws quite different things from those which it drew before.

Live '*à la bonne franquette*', without ceremony, as St. François de Sales used to say; by which he meant, do quite simply what you can, keeping within the limits of what you feel able to do.

Do the best you can, simply and promptly, according to your physical strength and the particular bent on your soul. That is all we have to do in this world, wherever or whatever we may be. It is with this that God creates holiness in us without our knowing anything about it.

We must follow our own path and not worry about the puddles into which we fall; otherwise we should never move on at all. The journey itself repairs the accidents into which it has led us; we dry ourselves, shake ourselves and on we go again. Tidy and timid travellers are never good travellers.

By 'the narrow way', our Lord never meant the way of narrowness of mind, of fear and trembling; those are bad ways. St. John said 'Fear drives out love'. And what could be worse than that! Remember that saying, 'Between the extremes of foolhardiness and timidity (choosing the path which has no risks), boldness is true wisdom', and add, 'true sense'. That is what the narrow way, the true way means. That is what this phrase expresses. Therefore, go resolutely forward.

X

HUMILITY

INDULGENCE TOWARDS OURSELVES

LET us content ourselves with being as little evil as we can. That done, all is well.

Perfection never exists apart from imperfection, just as good health cannot exist without our feeling effort, fatigue, heat or cold, hunger or thirst; yet none of those prevent the enjoyment of good health.

If you attempt to do all that is possible, all that is desirable, all that might be edifying, you will never succeed. Such an aim would indeed lack simplicity, humility, and frankness; and those three qualities are worth more than everything else to which you might aspire, however good your motives.

Perfection consists not in taking the safest course (sometimes quite the opposite) but in doing the least possible evil, having regard to our state of mind at the time and to the difficulties of our nature. It consists also in modestly holding fast to a very great simplicity, renouncing any course of action which although it either is, or appears to be more perfect in itself, would strain our powers.

I wish so much that you could get hold of the idea of what perfection in this world consists of. It is not like going up a great hill from which we see an ever-widening landscape, a greater horizon, a plain receding further and further into the distance. It is more like an overgrown path which we cannot find; we grope about; we are caught by brambles; we lose all sense of the distance covered; we do not know whether we are going round and round or whether we are advancing. We are certain only of one thing; that we desire to go on even though we are worn and tired. That is your life and you should rejoice greatly because of it, for it is a true life, serious and real, on which God opens His eyes and His heart.

We are far too apt to think of virtue as a broad, smooth road, whereas it is really a very rough and narrow one. It never becomes smooth or less uneven, until we observe that, in spite of all the jolting, we do manage to stay on it and even to advance a little, thanks to our Lord who holds us. Our confidence in Him, gained by experience, gives us a certain inward tranquillity in spite of the jolting. That is what is meant by the smooth road.

Our Lord does not plan interior splendours or exterior results for us in this world, but rather desolation, both within and without, to be endured as well as we can; that is the ideal. You must admit that from the moral point of view, this ideal is sublime and that it is admirably suited to human nature and to our earthly life. You will also observe that it is realized every day, which cannot be said of any other ideal.

It has been said that there are on the battlefield, defeats as glorious as victories. That is true also of the daily defeats of the soul in the struggle which we begin afresh every day, making new plans to do better and experimenting with new ideas and methods in order to succeed. That is what the Gospel declares: 'Happy is the servant whom when his Master cometh He shall find. . . .' Find how? Victorious? Triumphant? His task fully accomplished? No! Rather he who shall be found watching, vigilant, wide awake; that is to say looking after the things which are not going well and putting them right, time after time. That is our really great merit in the sight of God. Do not be surprised because I say *great*, even though in itself the merit is very small. It is great, because we are extremely weak and because God knows, as the Bible says, the clay of which we are made. God has ordered this world so that little things may become great, fitted as they are to our puny stature.

Let us put up with ourselves in charity and try to rule ourselves as we should like to rule others. That is to say, using towards ourselves much gentle and persuasive skill, which will turn us inside out as delicately as we turn a glove.

Use all your intelligence and experience in managing your own life, employing the tenderness you would expect to find in a being of ideal kindness. What I am asking you, in the name of our Lord, is to have charity towards yourself.

I know only too well the effect any disorder in the physical machinery has on the soul. Only the fatherly goodness of God knows how to compensate for this by attributing immense value to the sufferings and conflicts of the soul which labours under physical disabilities, and by assessing at zero almost all the failings and misdeeds which result more or less directly from bodily suffering.

Praise God! for I assure you that He is more compassionate than words can express. Be filled then with rejoicing; not because of your ills which are in themselves bad and must be cured, but because of the tenderness of God, who, with His fatherly and loving heart understands all your difficulties. Keep your inward peace therefore, however disturbed and distracted you may feel. Try to be as indulgent towards the poverty and faultiness of your soul as God Himself is.

To remain in a certain state of soul is to progress, just as agricultural progress on the land consists in doing the same work of the farm every day, ploughing the same number of furrows in the same way.

What I should like, therefore, in your case, is a feeling of rest. Say to yourself, 'I please God just as I am at this moment', and that even while taking your moral wretchedness into account. For there is no state of soul in which God does not make great allowances for our infirmities, thus showing His indulgence and His mercy. We must accept this, not proudly, but with loving gratitude and a growing sense of the loving-kindness of our Lord.

Moreover what I am asking of you in the name of your Saviour, is not stagnation, and you will realize this increasingly. For as you come more and more to accept the state of your soul as satisfactory, you will find greater freedom of spirit, greater joy and greater peace of soul. And all this will immensely strengthen you.

XI
SIMPLICITY

A PERFECT childlike simplicity puts us at once into intimate relationship with God, without any hindrance.

Let us try more and more to maintain in the depths of our souls the childlike simplicity and artlessness which our Lord asks and commands. If we cannot always behave in this way in the world, it is because intelligence and goodwill are often lacking in the world. It is never because of God, to whom we are never so pleasing as when we are really like little children before Him.

Simplicity is the final word as regards the true way of living. It is the lesson our Lord teaches us when He declares that the Kingdom of Heaven is for children and those who are childlike. Yet as with all childlike virtues, simplicity is easily practised in childhood, but still more easily lost afterwards. It is only by a long and roundabout route that we find it again, making it triumphantly and finally ours because we have won it for ourselves.

The concentration which we bring to bear on our interior conduct is like that which we bring to the learning of a new language. In your case it is now time for this intensity to cease and give place to interior simplicity, leaving the soul with great freedom of movement; in the same way that after we have spoken a foreign language for some time, we leave our words to look after themselves.

Is there not a stage when we are very careful about the details of grammar, and a later stage when we need think of nothing but of speaking freely and easily? It is the same with the growth of the spirit. After having studied ourselves deeply, we must then forget all about it, go straight ahead and do our best, trusting only to that simple instinct of straightforward wisdom which is the natural side, the truth of the Christian life. What perfection of good we reach in this way without realizing it. Just as, after our grammar lessons, we acquire a surprising fluency without thinking about it as soon as we aim at nothing but speaking naturally.

All those souls who seek God with great depth of desire are more or less entangled in their own aspirations. God is indeed pleased with them for having carried their goodwill and their love of virtue so far; but there comes a time when peace is found rather in humble, reasonable, confident simplicity. It is then that God allows the soul whose sufferings He has accepted, to feel His *consolation*—I do not say His *consolations*. We know instinctively that God is good and we never lose sight of that fact.

And so you in your turn must love our Lord with simplicity; that is to say with the entire conviction of your unending insufficiency, yet nevertheless, content to love Him thus. Do not attempt to compete with our Lord's love; you would necessarily be defeated in such an effort. Just go on with simplicity and humility as well as you can. That will be perfection. . . .

XII

ON FORGETTING OURSELVES
TO LOOK AT GOD

I CANNOT understand how in the presence of our Lord any one could go on thinking about himself, even if he were the last of men. Christ is our Saviour; He is our God; we can do nothing but fly to Him.

The time has come when you must no longer think of yourself—the poverty of your nature and your will—but only of the compassion and love which Jesus has for you. Rejoice in his thought; the more overjoyed the less you deserve it. That is all you have to do.

From every point of view we gain infinitely more by looking at our Lord, than by looking at ourselves. We shake off our faults more quickly and effectively when we adore our Lord than when we examine and criticize ourselves. On the human plane this is obvious, for we gain more by watching great and noble souls, than by shutting ourselves up in our own dreary dullness. We learn more and get more help from their simple vision than from all our own reasoning.

Our Lord gives to give and not to receive; very little suffices Him. Therefore accept everything from Him, however unworthy, however ungrateful, however 'unrepaying' you may be. Receive again and again. Rejoice in receiving, without afterthought. Ask again and always, and if possible, for ever more and more. Think always of that which you receive, never of that which you give. This is a far better way of entering into the love of our Lord and acquiring a boundless confidence in Him, than by looking at yourself and thinking of what you can do for Him. He is more interesting than you are, even to yourself. Look at Him therefore and lose sight of yourself. I assure you that this is the best thing you can do and will have excellent results.

The soul gains very little from looking at itself. Such an occupation gives rise only to discouragement, preoccupation, distress, uncertainty, and illusion.

Looking at our Lord, on the contrary, does us good
and we are gradually transfigured by His personality
and by the spirit of imitation. Christian teachers
ask a soul to look at itself only when it requires to
be brought low, to be humiliated and frightened,
sobered in its view of itself and of the world. But that
is all that the soul can get out of itself. It sees that it
must change, must go forward; but how? There is
only one way; to contemplate the perfect soul and
heart of our Lord; to study Him in those pages of the
Gospel which touch us most. Such a vision works on
us through example, through teaching, and through
the power of His Divine attraction which surpasses all
things.

What is so beautiful in these things of God is their
simplicity, their childlike truth, their infinitely wise
and gentle loving kindness, their perfect adaptability
to our poor human nature, their real and practical
beauty without strain or ambitious aims. They are, in
short, the secret of the heart of God for man.

XIII
LOVE OF GOD

SPEND your time in loving our Lord as simply as possible and without any afterthought, just because He is the ideal and He belongs to you. He is so gentle and humble of heart that it is pure delight to talk to Him quite frankly, without any spiritual tension, in complete simplicity.

Never think for a moment of what you are when you contemplate God and our Lord. See Him only as He who is most to be loved and most loving. That thought alone will wipe out all your sins, even though they be great. Love of God is salvation itself, and we love God naturally by His grace, because He is the very ideal of that which attracts the heart and the affections. He answers exactly to that which we long to love without measure.

What I should like to see springing up in your life would be an easier, more confident, more spontaneous love for Jesus, whom you love so much in reality, but with whom you have not yet learnt to practise an absolutely free and childlike intimacy. If you would only say to yourself that Jesus is absolutely lovable, quite apart from all that you are or are not, and that in consequence you have always the right to love Him in your heart, even if you cannot always succeed in loving Him by acts; then you would be in the Truth. If you would say to yourself firmly that Jesus is unbelievably and unimaginably loving, and that His love does not vary with the variations of your soul, you would be in the Truth. For real affection is never dependent on the fluctuations of those whom it loves; what may vary, according to our feelings and acts, is the satisfaction of our Lord. But we must never confuse 'to be satisfied' with 'to be loved'.

In order that this grace may have its full expression and expansion in you, God asks only one thing and that is that you should be on close and friendly terms with Him, without fear; without exception; I was about to say, without ceremony. The fact is that we do not love fully and with our whole being, unless we can be on the same terms with God as we are with our own souls. Then our love is full, true, deep, whole, indestructible, and as it were, instinctive. We lack nothing; we are hampered by nothing; in everything we enjoy the happiness of an absolute intimacy, a complete familiarity.

Do not keep accounts with our Lord and say, 'I did Him such an injury, therefore He owes me such a grudge. He cannot be on good terms with me because I have not paid Him this or that; it would not be just otherwise'.

Go bankrupt! Let our Lord love you without justice! Say frankly, 'He loves me because I do not deserve it; that is the wonderful thing about Him; and that is why I, in my turn, love Him as well as I can without worrying whether I deserve to be allowed to love Him. He loves me although I am not worthy; I love Him without being worthy to love'.

I know no other way of loving God. Therefore burn your account books! You may say, 'I love Him and yet I constantly offend Him. How can these two things go together?' You actually ask me how these two things can go together in human nature, in this nature of ours which is continuously full of contradictions?

You will always offend God in some way; that is only one reason the more for making amends, both to yourself and to Him, by loving Him always and for evermore.

XIV
CONFIDENCE IN GOD

ABOVE everything else you must develop confidence in the love which our Lord bears you. That must become your chief virtue. Consequently you must practise gratitude, tranquillity, joy, and affection; and this most of all when things are not going well with you, when something sinful and warped gets hold of you. Because it is just then that we most need to remember this love which does not forsake us, but calls us back.

If you base your confidence in God on the thought that He loves you on account of your merits, then your confidence in Him will always be very feeble. But once you base your confidence and certitude of being loved on the free and permanent and incessant gift of grace, then your confidence will be sure and strong.

When bit by bit you have given up scrutinizing your soul and the Christian life according to a mass of petty theological rules; when you have simply thrown yourself at the feet of our Lord, following the impulse of your particular nature and grace; when you have done this tranquilly, without strain and without afterthought, sure of that which is most real—*then* you will have made a great step forward and truly found God.

Let us go to Him who is goodness itself with a simplicity of confidence. I beg you to banish all fear, all apprehension and to incline to nothing but peace, frankness, and joy. Love our Lord tranquilly in the knowledge that He is infinitely lovable; that is all. After that it is for Him to take charge of us, and He will not be found wanting.

What ought to make us most afraid is our weakness, our cowardice, our detestable nature; but we escape this fear precisely by casting ourselves on our Lord, relying on Him to save us, in spite of everything.

I order, I command, I beg, I insist, I entreat you to lay aside all fear of God. It is ridiculous. You do not understand what God is like. He is the most sympathetic of friends, always biased in our favour, always most indulgent, most generous. Everything which has represented God to you as other than this, is a legacy from Judaism and Paganism. What fear have you of the Judgement? Would you like to be judged by me at the Gates of Heaven? Would you feel confident that I should be lenient? Of course you would! Very well then! God will be more lenient still, because He is better than I am, and loves you, as is His right, in a still more fatherly way. This is absolutely true and you must change your ideas about this completely. You must feel nothing but confidence in the infinite mercy of God.

I tell you as solemnly as if our Lord said it Himself, that you must cease to have any fear of Him, for fear grieves Him. When you are in any trouble; even if alas! you have brought it on yourself, throw yourself boldly at the feet of our Saviour, at the feet of rescuing Love; hide yourself in this sanctuary and be so ravished by God's gentleness and tenderness, that you come to love and know Him a little better. This is what He asks of you, and this is the result He means your difficulties to produce in you. You will afterwards imitate His compassion as well as you can towards others, thus modelling yourself, your heart and soul, on Jesus Christ, becoming His true ministering servant.

The wonderful works of God are not always revealed to us. It is through events that they are revealed and we may be sure of the results. This is what is called the test of fidelity.

Our Lord watches over His own. Those who seek Him always find, under one form or another, all that they need for the wise guidance of their souls. It is above all in this form of blessing that God manifests Himself.

I have constantly experienced that in my own case, in the most diverse and unforeseen circumstances. I have always found our Lord providing, in the nick of time, that which is best for the training of the soul. Always have absolute confidence in this for the Gospel proclaims it: 'I am the Good Shepherd; my sheep hear my voice. I lead them! I know them each by name and they follow Me!'

As soon as we become observant we see at once that our Lord is our true and chief Director, who, without our knowledge, has arranged matters in such a way that our lives turn out quite differently from what we should have expected; infinitely better for our salvation and glory than we should ever have dared to hope.

God gradually takes away our supports, whether of nature or of grace. With the passing of time we are apt to become aware of the menace of finding ourselves left alone. What resource do you suppose there is, save that of making up our minds to put ourselves completely and delightedly into the hands of God? That is what we must do, casting a glance of absolute confidence towards Him: a confidence founded solely on His goodness. Do not argue with Him. Tell Him frankly that all your fears will not frighten, nor all your unworthiness intimidate you, when it comes to trusting Him; that in spite of everything, you do trust Him and, moreover, with peace, serenity, and love, both in season and out of season.

XV
GOD LOVES US

How happy God is in loving us! Like parents who adore their children. It is really just like that and it is *grand*, and just what we should expect of God. It is also necessary for us, poor little creatures that we are. Praise God!

Be bold enough always to believe that God is on your side and wholly yours, whatever you may think of yourself.

As for that which is beyond your strength, be absolutely certain that our Lord loves you, devotedly and individually: loves you just as you are. How often that conviction is lacking even in those souls who are most devoted to God! They make repeated efforts to love Him, they experience the joy of loving, and yet how little they know, how little they realize, that God loves them incomparably more than they will ever know how to love Him. Think of this and say to yourself 'I am loved by God more than I can either conceive or understand'. Let this fill all your soul and all your prayer and never leave you. You will soon see that this is the way to find God. It contains the whole of St. John's teaching: 'As for us, we have believed in the love which God has for us.' I have asked God to teach me this and now I understand it. I know that it is the true way, the best way and the way which is so often lacking in souls. Find it without delay.

Accustom yourself to the wonderful thought that God loves you with a tenderness, a generosity, and an intimacy which surpasses all your dreams. Give yourself up with joy to a loving confidence in God and have courage to believe firmly that God's action towards you is a masterpiece of partiality and love. Rest tranquilly in this abiding conviction.

The thing which may for long prevent the soul from thus accepting our Lord, is that it forgets to think of Him always and above all as compassionate. Yet in everything, that is the first idea we must try to have about Him. We shall be quite differently affected by His great splendour if we first realize that He to whom it belongs and who offers it to us, is

compassionate beyond all words. How gladly shall
we then rejoice in His Divine splendours! For they
are the splendours of the All-Compassionate, the
Intimate, and the Familiar God!

We must think of our Lord as loving us more than
any one else, upholding us even when we are ready
mercilessly to condemn ourselves; think of Him as
being our other self, bolder in approval and more
ready to rejoice over us than we are ourselves. That is
the ideal of fatherhood, of friendship and of love.
When we know our Lord thus, we know Him well
and every thing is easy. The terrible God, the angry,
exacting, narrow God, has completely disappeared.
We are attracted to our Lord and profoundly reassured. And so we love with confidence and joy.

Rejoice that you are what you are; for our Lord
loves you very dearly. He loves the whole of you, just
as you are. In spite therefore of all your troubles,
troubles about people and things, remain at peace.
Drop all your spiritual anxieties and do not goad
yourself to efforts which will only overburden and
overstrain you. Such efforts are not only useless but
even harmful, for they war against that peace which
the Christ-God demands: the peace which, in this
world, must always exist in the midst of our imperfections: the imperfections of things, the imper-

fections of people. Imitate the calm of the sailor standing on the deck of his ship, which is in itself never still: or that of the man who walks quietly through the city, indifferent to the noise and the winding of the streets, picking his way through the people and the traffic. . . .

Be reassured and comforted. Rejoice from the bottom of your heart at this assurance I am giving you, as if it came from our Lord Himself. For it is only in this blessed certitude that you will find that freedom of spirit which is absolutely necessary. I implore you in God's name, not to think of Him as hard to please, but rather as generous beyond all that you can ask or think. Get rid, once and for all, of the idea that God is displeased or intolerant towards our weakness. The truth is exactly the opposite. Accept that fact and act upon it.

You have not grasped the right idea of God and of His service. You always come back to the thought that God must be dissatisfied, which is not so. Remember that it is our souls, yes! our own souls! which are God's joy: not on account of what they do for Him, but on account of what He does for them. All that He asks of them is gladly to accept His kindness, His generosity, His tolerance, His fatherly love. Let your adoration of God, therefore, take this form and do not

worry any more about what you are or are not. You
are the object of His mercy. Be satisfied with that
and think only of that.

The essence of the matter is that our Lord loves you
dearly. The more keenly therefore, you realize that
the weakness is of your own nature, even of your own
will, the more you must adore Him. For in spite of
everything, we *are* the weak creatures whom our
Lord loves, and loves deeply, with a love worthy of
that name, which to Him is no idle word.

You want to compete with His affection before you
have understood it; that is your mistake. You are like
a child who wants to help his mother before allowing
himself to be trained by her. You are like St. Peter;
he wanted to wash his Master's feet, but refused to
allow his Master to wash his feet. He did not
understand. Our Lord showed him his mistake with
the clear and decisive sharpness of a friend: 'Peter! if I
do not do this, and if you will not let me do it, you
have no part in me!' And St. John, who knew all the
depth and tenderness of God's love, was constantly
ravished by the thought, 'He loved us first!'

Come then! show a little deference to our Lord and
allow Him to go first. Let Him love you a great deal,

a very great deal, long before you have succeeded in loving Him, even a little, as you would wish to love Him.

That is all I ask of you, and all that our Lord asks of you.

Say to yourself very often about everything that happens, 'God loves me! What joy!' And reply boldly, 'And I truly love Him too!' Then go quite simply about all that you have to do and do not philosophize any more. For these two phrases are beyond all thought and do more for us than any thought could do; they are all-sufficing.

XVI
GOD WITHIN US

OUR true light and power lie in the hidden source of interior grace in which God springs up ceaselessly within our souls. The soul is saturated with God's own life, His presence, His activity, His inspiration, His encouragement and the radiance of His presence. 'The Master is here and calls for you!' He speaks to you. It is very rare for the interior Master not to speak in the depths of the soul. The tone is varied as in the Gospel, but it is always Divine. Nobler and loftier than ours, it is at the same time simpler, humbler, and more natural. No one speaks that language except our Lord Himself in His Gospel. Thus we each have at will the private, special, secret companionship of God, of the Divine Persons. What delight, what joy this is! Their discourse never ceases, yet the eternal theme is always new and never wearies us.

This is what our Lord asks of you; to be content to live with Him without anxiety, without any strain after perfection. Rest content with the knowledge that He is His own Person, with the Father and the Holy Spirit, is in your soul, substantially, really, literally; that He does everything you do with you, from the humblest duties to the highest. Your whole devotional life should consist in this companionship, accepted without ceremony, without intellectual or emotional effort, simply possessed and enjoyed, in perfect calmness and tranquillity. You are to say nothing to our Lord except that which comes of itself, and that in the most homely words. Never stop for a moment to ask whether or why you are worthy of this simple companionship on such a footing. Simply practise it; that is all. As for the other things, such as acts of external devotion, they are only patterns, superimposed on this simple friendship. They should neither ruffle nor disturb its inward life.

Do not be distressed that the frequency of your Communions is to be reduced. What would be distressing would be to be deprived of them by your own free and voluntary act, or, by some one else's futility. But to be deprived of Communion by a definite order does not deprive us of its fruits nor even of its joy and consolation. Our Saviour is not bound to any particular means of grace and does not necessarily need the channel of Communion to give our souls the

nourishment He desires to give them. God gives
Himself generously by interior grace, by the habitual
indwelling in us of the three Divine Persons, a fact of
which we have often spoken. It even happens that the
soul, with less emphasis on external things, develops
the excellent habit of dwelling with greater vividness
and reality on the constant indwelling of God within
her. That is a perpetual Communion, a Communion
which continues even when the sacramental one
ceases. It is the joy of joys. It is that which God wishes
you to enjoy.

The mystery of grace which works in us and which
works more fully in souls given to God, is in a sense a
copy of the Mystery of the Incarnation. By grace
Jesus takes possession of our personality and fills it
with His Divinity. Let us therefore never leave out
the part played by our humanity in the mystery of
grace; a mystery which comprises the whole Christian
life and even more, the religious life. Let us take
ourselves as we are and put our whole selves gladly at
the service, both interior and exterior, of our Lord.
That which He wishes to possess of us by grace, is our
very self, our own personal self. As He says in the
Gospel, 'I call my sheep by name'. He desires to make
use of us by grace as He made use of His own nature
in the Incarnation.

Great God! what tranquil and abiding joy it is to
know that it is Jesus Himself who stirs within us and
to know that our whole duty lies only in keeping
ourselves free and supple, in order that He may act in
us.

But what happens when the soul becomes stubborn,
when it stiffens itself, gets confused, discouraged, and
frightened?

Well! we can only put that too at the interior and
exterior service of Jesus and say, 'Lord! you wish to
make use of all that is going on within me. Then take
it, Lord, and use it. It has nothing more to do with
me. You wish to be disturbed within me; you wish to
dwell without feeling in me; you wish to fight within
me; to fight with great difficulty? Well! if it is really
You who thus turn everything upside down within
me—then come and do! I will help. I will try to bear
all that is unavoidable, and use every means which can
bring the struggle to an end'.

The intimacy of the soul with our Lord provides
our true nourishment, our true home, however much
circumstances change. This is the blessed truth our
Lord tries to teach us through all our troubles; to
make us realize that the power of Jesus is the only
power which holds us so firmly that it never fails. He

wants to be all in all to us: He alone can be that and He is it to perfection. It is a great joy to realize this completely. How faithful this hidden and intimate attachment of our Lord is to our souls! What a foretaste of Paradise amidst the troubles of earth!

XVII
INTERIOR DIFFICULTIES

CONSOLATIONS and sensible desires are only means for training the will and forming permanent habits. As soon as the will is fixed, consolations and sensible enthusiasm become mere luxuries and we can wait for them with the more patience.

We are never so near God as when we have to get on as well as we can without the consolation of feeling His presence. It is not when the child is with his mother that she is most anxious for his welfare. It is when the child thinks he is alone that his mother is most compassionate and thinks of him most tenderly. It is the same with God and ourselves.

You ask me, 'Why does God do this?' Because what matters most to Him is not that He should do the work Himself; that would and always will be easy for Him. His real desire is to make us do something. By concealing Himself, He can often persuade us to go on by ourselves and to exert more real virtue. But does this prove that He does not love us? Quite the contrary.

When He does not allow you to be aware of His presence for a long time, for longer than you feel you can bear it, it is because He relies on you. And if He does rely on you, it is because He knows He can do so. . . .

Be at peace then, and simply remember not to allow yourself to be distracted by things which merely hover in the back of your mind. . . .

Do not worry about your feelings, but act as if you had those which you would like to have. This is not done by making a mental effort, nor by seeking to feel that which you do not feel; but by simply doing without the feeling you have not got and behaving exactly as if you had it. When you realize that lack of feeling does not hinder reality, you will no longer put your trust in your own thoughts, but in that which our Lord makes you do. We are very slow in realizing this, but we must do so. Come now! have a little of that tranquil fearlessness which makes for good, without so much thought and scrupulousness. Behave just as naturally as if you were coming downstairs!

We must not consider that which comes from our natural impulses as being part of our real selves. We are not responsible for our feelings but for our decisions. What does it matter if our sensible nature feels upset? If we act rightly, then all is well. You would probably rather not experience those perpetual contradictions in yourself of which St. Paul also complained. But you will remember that our Lord did not agree with him and left him as he was. This is what St. Paul meant when he said, 'Unhappy man that I am! The good that I would I do not and the evil that I would not, that I do!'

In other words, we have not the characters we should like to have and we have those we should like not to have. What are we to do?

Instead of chasing after them, we must simply do without them and be satisfied with acting rightly, without wanting to feel inclined to such action.

The root of many of your troubles is the desire to have only good inclinations. That is neither necessary nor possible. In countless ways we shall always feel ourselves to be wicked, unstable and unreasonable. We must realize that this is our nature and not our real personality; not our true, deliberate and voluntary desire: not the goal of our efforts.

The best thing is not so much to see our Lord do away with our difficulties as to see Him sustain us

through them. If we were without difficulties might
we not think that they would perhaps return and
destroy our serenity?

Instead of which, when we realize to what a degree
our Lord always gets us out of our difficulties, in spite
of our anxieties, weaknesses, and failings, then we
begin to acquire assurance and serenity even in the
midst of our troubles. Thus the difficulty loses its
sting and venom; it does not pierce our soul so deeply
because we know that our Lord always opens some
way of escape, probably an unexpected one, by which
He rescues us from the extreme danger we feared.

Therefore when you say, 'I have difficulties, either
within or without', you are doubtless looking on the
black side of things. Yet it is really all to the good, in
that it forces you to see that you are carrying on all the
same, and that in consequence Our Lord is ultimately
helping you to cross the torrent. . . .

Our Lord is with us in all our troubles and always
gives us sufficient help to carry us through.

Smile and even laugh at yourself when you feel all
this inner hubbub going on in you. It is the childish
language of nature; plaintive, fearful, unreasonable;
we always have it with us. It is a splendid habit to
laugh inwardly at yourself. It is the best way of
regaining your good humour and of finding God
without further anxiety.

What you need to realize once and for all is that a good state of soul can, in this world, go hand in hand with a feeling of deep inward disharmony. This feeling is nothing more than an accurate recognition of the true state of human life, which is not a state of triumph and splendour but of confusion and cloudiness. . . .

Our Lord acts as do Alpine guides. We are roped to Him with a rope which He has Himself made fast; and while He steadily follows the rough tracks by which He wishes to lead us, we seem to be more often on the ground than on our feet. We appear to be suspended over crevasses which do not however engulf us. We go on through the mist and the icy cold; the path is strange rather than picturesque. But all this does not prevent us from reaching the summits.

That is the true picture of our route and of our progress. From the time we think we are going to find the main route, we worry about not being on it already. But as soon as we realize, like the Swiss, that we are on the native tracks of the country, we instinctively adapt ourselves and are no more troubled by them than an Alpine shepherd who goes up and down them every day.

Do not be distressed by lack of fervour and consolations. These will come in their own time and their own way. Our Lord wants you to become mature, and maturity needs these periods of obscurity, of disillusionment and boredom. Maturity comes when we have at last realized that we must love our Lord simply and freely in spite of our own horrible unworthiness and of the unworthiness of nearly everything around us. Then a new and lasting Incarnation of our Lord takes place in our souls, as it were. He begins to live a new life within us in the very midst of the misery of the world.

That is why the greatest Saints have always shown the perfect combination of nearness to our Lord on the one hand, and a deep sense of their own unworthiness and weakness on the other. We should like to love our Lord perfectly; but the only really perfect way is to love Him in a simple, human way. I assure you that it is a very excellent way and, in the eyes of the angels, a most perfect and touching sight.

They see our Lord loved by men, who do not for that reason cease to be men, and they see our Lord loving men who are nevertheless nothing but men. Is there anything on earth more beautiful than that?

XVIII
SUFFERING

Do not let us fear things too much, for we often suffer more from the things we fear than from those which really come to pass. And what good does it do, seeing that when evils come, they bring with them strength to enable us to accept them; a strength which we do not have in advance. We are more in the Truth and therefore have more power in the face of real ills than in the face of those which do not yet exist. Be very definite about this, as indeed about everything, for God has made our nature for that which is, and not for that which our spirit creates for itself. Apply this principle to everything and you will experience strength and joy, life and truth; you will feel the power and beauty of all that really is, of all that really finds its true end and is in tune with what God has made.

Why make a misery of those troubles which belong to our earthly state and which happen to every one? We may dislike them, but there is nothing to be surprised about in that, and after all there are other much worse evils. A sturdy common sense is always necessary. People generally think less ill of us than we believe. They like us in reality more than they appear to do or than we wish. Instead of 'ill-will' we should say 'lack of goodwill' (through narrowness, stupidity, ignorance, or weakness). It is in the midst of all this that we have to live in this world and none of it has ever prevented us from living. It serves us right and though it may not do us any particular good, yet it is not 'death itself'.

There are extraordinary trials which God allows in order that they may be fought, weakened, rejected. The most marvellous of all, the Passion of our Lord, was one of these. Our Lord endured terror and weariness to the point of the bloody sweat. Well! He begged His Father to take away the cup. An angel came from Heaven to comfort Him and He rose up and felt no more fear. Under the weight of the Cross He fell. Then He accepted help in carrying it. He was thirsty. Then He asked for something to drink; and as the drink was bitter, He did not want it. In that mob of blind and hostile souls He wanted to have His mother, St. Mary Magdalene and St. John nearest to Him, that is to say, those who were best able to console Him.

We will pray that God may for ever spare you such sufferings. For although it is good to have passed through them, it is nevertheless in line with all the instincts God has given us, to plead for exemption. *Christus mortuus, jam non moritur;* before the final resurrection there is something noble and beautiful in the resurrection which, even in this life, follows on pain and suffering.

The supreme object of life is not to escape trials, even though this is an alleviation which we often feel we need. Yet if this is denied us we have to fall back on something else. We have to try to understand the trial, to see the point of it and to know how best to face it. It is on this last point, how to rule ourselves in times of trial, that, with God's help, I want to help you. For this we must use every means at our disposal.

I note in particular that you have wished to 'love' suffering. I was about to say, 'But why, so long as you bear it?' That is all our Lord asked for Himself in His agony, in His Passion, on the Cross. His human nature too, shrank at the horror of suffering. 'Father! that the cup may pass from me!' And the bloody sweat! What a horror of suffering we see there. 'Father! why hast Thou forsaken me?' Yet Our Lord did quite simply what you will do too. He bore it.

When God destines us for suffering, it is far better to go through it, even though we often fail and meet with spiritual reverses, than not to have had the experience; to remain untouched because we have not suffered. Why? Because the merit of suffering, (whose value in the eyes of God who is so good and tender, is beyond all measure,) far exceeds if willed and accepted all that we could lose by any weaknesses which arose from such suffering. It is rather like the merit of those who have gone through the test of life. With all their faults, they rank higher in glory than those perfectly pure children who died directly after baptism. As therefore God has allowed you to suffer, you are more pleasing in His eyes, even though interiorly or exteriorly sinful, than if you were absolutely sinless, thanks to not having had to bear suffering. Praise God! All this is really true without the slightest doubt!

Such trials are not experienced without injuring the soul in many ways and that is why they are a higher kind of suffering. Yet this is not quite a fair way of putting it and tends to make us more aware of our partial failures and our natural weaknesses than of the great victory (or if you prefer it the great sacrament) with which suffering has crowned us; so that we may bear some likeness to Christ on the Cross and be marked out to share this supreme glory with Him.

God keeps you on a short rein like a horse which is being broken in. He uses the whip as though He meant to make you kick, yet He has a firm hold on the reins which force you to obey His will. Always be very open to receive any guidance of this kind. These are the most valuable encounters of life and are those which we later recognize as being the experiences which have given us the most solid hopes of salvation. We can say with David, 'I bless Thee, Lord, above all for those evil days which Thou hast let me see'.

God crushes you when you are already down; that does seem the last straw! But do not be distressed! He loves you, and that in no ordinary measure. Love Him therefore this way; feel the horror of each blow, even of each pin-prick, but at the same time know with joy and adoration and absolute certainty that each blow is really a mark of His love. That is the truth. I swear it!

Our tears must not be bitter for God is kind, kind to those we love, kind to us. Neither must we let our troubles embitter us, for God has great compassion on our weakness and great consideration for our littleness. The last thing He wants to do is to crush us. If,—as with His Son, 'in whom He was well-pleased',—He allows us to be broken when we are already down, worn out by our infirmities, then surely it is in order that we may learn confidence and fearlessness.

Rejoice to think that after having recovered yourself in the midst of interior pain and difficulty, you will be able to help others in their turn. No one can help save he who has suffered. God destines you for this. Let this be your joy.

Natures like yours, which have had to struggle, are of great use in the world especially in these times. Some day they will recognize this after having long thought their sufferings and efforts of no use.

It is not only by action that we are of use. Let us preserve our desire for activity, but do not let us be unfair to an even deeper and more sublime ministry: the ministry of suffering. Let us realize that it is a great ministry with a power which nothing can resist.

How much I feel for your suffering. Yet, as in everything, do not accept it or dwell on it, except in so far as our human nature in its present state can find goodness, tenderness, and sympathy in it. Even our tears should be consoling and comforting. God, the splendour of all fatherly goodness, wants us to take from things only that which will help us and to reject everything which will harm us. 'Deliver us from evil', is the last petition of the Lord's Prayer, a petition which came from the very soul of Christ. If we based our Christianity on the belief that God wants us only to take happiness from everything around us, what delight it would give Him, what homage it would be to His goodness, His deep love towards us. Give to God then and to yourself, this real, strong and just happiness, even in your suffering. Face every encounter with this gift of seeing 'happiness' in God.

I have suffered enough in the course of many years to have an intense and profound horror of suffering in itself and in all the burdens it lays on the soul. On the other hand, with what compassion Infinite Goodness surrounds all those who have been crushed by suffering. It is a debt due to them for it is not in vain that God is good. He needs to be, and He will be, satisfied. In this life we shall have conquered that terrible difficulty, crucifixion. We shall no longer come before God with the fear of having escaped this most painful condition of salvation. That is indeed a triumph and an asset. In thought we can often prostrate ourselves with an immense feeling of confidence and of the help of grace, for such a benefit received. We can and should think of our past ills in the joyful light of the Biblical description of the elect: All suffering passed, joy only remaining.

XIX
ILLNESS

THOSE who do not understand our suffering nor appreciate its handicaps are much to be pitied. This lack of understanding always exists and distinguishes those in good health, however charitable they may be, from those in bad health.

Do not be unhappy at being left alone with your sufferings, nobody appearing to be interested or to understand. Look after yourself, take reasonable precautions and do not worry about the attitude of other people. Keep your tranquillity and believe that God will use all this for good.

I am delighted to know that you are a little better in health. That is very important. Do your best to keep and increase this blessing which is, even supernaturally, of the first importance. It is one of the mistakes mankind still makes, that it does not give this blessing the place God has given it in His creation, both natural and supernatural. It was our Lord's desire not to be ill and He cured all the sick who were brought to Him. God eliminates illness through the growth of knowledge and of human wisdom. We must follow the same course. Nothing is gained by overworking; that is quite clear. We pay too dearly for it; we must therefore never do it knowingly.

Do your very best to increase your physical strength. It is one of those things without which you will never achieve stability.

Give yourself, and whenever possible accept from others, everything which may alleviate your suffering or improve your health. The Divine order of life wills this and such care is neither a defect nor a softness. I know what I am talking about.

While accepting provisionally this influence of the physical on the moral, we must nevertheless try to obviate it, for it is not an ideal state. In order to do this be a little more tolerant towards yourself; do not try to force yourself to constant good efforts, whether interior or exterior, when you feel that tired nature implores you, as a poor cab-horse might ask its driver, to leave it alone and have pity on its impotence.

Take care of yourself in order to recover what God has charged us to seek: that is normal health in accordance with the laws of our being. 'Our Father, may Thy will be done on earth'—that is to say in the regular order of nature: 'as it is done in Heaven'—that is to say in the supernatural order of the elect. Let us observe natural laws in this world as the elect observe celestial laws in Heaven! Let us get well!

I am truly sorry that you are suffering so grievously and I sympathize with all my heart in this real martyrdom of which I too have experience. It is a great trial because it never stops; it affects everything and most of the time it inevitably destroys the mainspring of vitality which is so great a counterpoise to illness. Yet we must not complicate or aggravate this situation by misunderstanding it. You must first of all reduce the physical distress as far as you can. Allow, with infinite indulgence, your poor exhausted nature to go its own pace. Prudence in this is wisdom. For if you try to mortify a nature already physically broke, you will only increase its weakness and its difficulties to such a degree that in the end you will be obliged to give in much more than would otherwise be necessary. Therefore on this point, as on all others, great breadth and wisdom.

This depression, this feeling of being at the end of your tether, is merely a physical sensation and does not arise from any weakness or softness of the soul. Bear patiently this feeling of being quite without vigour, enthusiasm, or energy. Be content to go very gently without feeling that you must take yourself to task. When vitality returns, accept it, but meanwhile do not strain after it.

Your soul has not deteriorated at all; on the contrary. It is the physical and external conditions which have changed. You no longer derive from them the same impressions as before. You can therefore no longer feel the same towards them. A good walker who has walked all day, feels no desire to walk in the evening. Has his nature changed? No! It is the conditions within which he acts that have changed. He still likes walking, but he has no desire to walk in conditions which are unsuitable.

The state of your health is largely responsible for the experiences of your soul. And far from such apparent defects being charged against your soul and your conscience, they are, before God, your defence, your justification and your glory. You will therefore not blame yourself when bad health makes you feel out of temper. It is not a defect but a merit. Say to yourself that if you were in better health you would be more at one with God, happier with God *in appearance*, but less so in reality.

What matters most of all is that you should not take this lassitude, this fear and this physical disability as coming in any way from your soul or from spiritual things. I have had great difficulty myself in getting used to doing just what I am telling you to do. But by repeating it to oneself, one accomplishes it in the end. If you are troubled, discontented, dull, anxious or fearful, say to yourself, 'No! That does not come from my spirit! It does not come from me! Come! my soul! Be at peace! Be happy! Reassure yourself! Be kind to yourself! Do not seriously impute any of this to yourself. Know that you live with God, that you are on good terms with Him, or what is even better, that God is on good terms with you. Rejoice and be strong, my soul! And send packing all this unhappy view of things which only weakness of body and constant ill-health have conjured up.'

XX
DEATH

THE life of man is by no means limited to its short passage through this world. Death is only an illusion which hides from us the continuing development of life. And, moreover, we are generally dead in many respects before the actual moment which completes our transformation. Interior changes gradually make us realize that, in spite of all our vicissitudes, we are indeed immortal, with a life, an endless activity, which death does not cut short: far from it.

Whatever time therefore, we may have lost in this world through circumstances which have checked our activity, is a small matter compared to the life without end which dwells in us and which will easily catch us up later on.

Life limited by death? Nonsense! That is a great mistake. Death hardly counts; it is a mere appearance; we already have eternal life and that reflection should give us great tranquillity, as those who feel themselves to be eternal.

Do not therefore be afraid of death. It is the flowering of life, the consummation of union with God.

Bossuet, who never spoke lightly, explained to his nuns that for them, the terror of death did not exist. In as much as death is an occasion of alarm to the natural man, in so much more is it an occasion of joy to those souls who have given themselves to Christ who welcomes them so eagerly. He comes to them in festal spirit and with power, making these last moments the easiest and safest in life.

Do not be anxious about death even though you feel it to be imminent and have every reason for despair, but give yourself up all the more to the mercy of God. No one, not even the Saints, can do anything else. They can only confide themselves hopefully to God'. Death is frightening only when it is far off, and it is useless to think of it from our present standpoint. I have seen many people die, and not one of them had the slightest fear of death once it was there.

St. Theresa says that nothing can give a Christian soul a better idea of death than ecstasy: *that* surely is not frightening! Bossuet, who was more severe, recommended priests who ministered to the dying only to talk to them of their coming joy, and to help them to enter at once into that state of peace and rest, of confidence and joy, which was so soon to open before them. Just as, when we return home after a long absence and first catch sight of our own country and our own home, we experience in anticipation, the joy and delight of arrival. . . .

There is also experience to help us and it is difficult to express the peace and joy with which the most ordinary but truly Christian souls meet death.

When you think you are going to die say to yourself, 'So much the better! I am about to behold the Adorable!'

What great festivals the first Christians made of the death of their martyrs, and that through their deaths often caused them irreparable loss! Irreparable at least, according to human ideas. But what do those to whom we are bound in Christ Jesus not do for us, once they have entered into the fullness of their power in God?